KidLit-O

What's So Great About Sacagawea?

A Biography of Sacagawea Just for Kids!

Max Tanner

KidLit-O Books

www.kidlito.com

© 2014. All Rights Reserved.

Table of Contents

About KidCaps

KidLit-O is an imprint of BookCaps™ that is just for kids! Each month BookCaps will be releasing several books in this exciting imprint. Visit are website or like us on Facebook to see more!

To add your name to our mailing list, visit this link: **http://www.kidlito.com/mailing-list.html**

[1] Image source: http://upload.wikimedia.org/wikipedia/commons/f/fd/Detail_Lewis _%26_Clark_at_Three_Forks.jpg

Introduction

The weather had been more or less calm for several days, but this afternoon it was obvious that things would be different. Young Sacagawea, only about 17 years old, looked at the scene around her with concern in her eyes. At his spot near the rudder of the small white boat, her husband Toussaint was equally worried. But unlike Sacagawea, his eyes were filled with a special kind of terror at the thought of riding out a storm being out in the middle of a wide and fast moving river. After all, Toussaint didn't know how to swim. If the wind picked up and tipped the boat, he would probably be the first to go overboard.

Toussaint looked around with sharp movements of his head, resembling a deer that was being stalked by a wolf. Taking deep breaths to keep herself from doing the same, Sacagawea noticed that her infant son Jean Baptiste was wiggling around in the cradleboard he was fastened to, which in turn was strapped onto the back of his mother. Could he sense the danger they were facing? Saying a few soft words to calm both herself and her son as the dark clouds of the storm moved towards them, Sacagawea noticed that the tips of the waves on the river were turning white as the stiff breeze pushed them higher and higher.

The winds of the oncoming storm grew stronger, and Sacagawea knew that the small party was about to have some trouble. She had seen storms like these before and knew their power. Barely one month had passed since she set out alongside her husband on this historic journey to the Pacific Ocean. They joined a group of about thirty men who had been sent by President Thomas Jefferson to explore the massive territory acquired by the United States from France during the Louisiana Purchase. The trip had sounded like it would be an exciting adventure back when she and Toussaint talked about it, sitting in the safety of their home. But now, feeling exposed out in the middle of the Musselshell River, Sacagawea was wondering if it had all been a mistake.

The storm was almost on top of them now, and the winds were blowing stronger than ever. Looking at her husband, something became clear to Sacagawea. Her husband Toussaint, who had been acting as the navigator during their trek up this tributary of the Musselshell River, was beginning to panic. His wide eyes and jerky movements betrayed his fears and the fact that he didn't have any idea of how to control his boat during stormy weather.

Toussaint's own fear of drowning amplified his terror and he couldn't stop imagining what would happen if he were to be thrown overboard. As the wind picked up the waters on the river got rougher, the boat began to rock from side to side. Each tilt of the boat felt more extreme than the last, and it wasn't long before some of the icy cold river water found its way into the craft with each dip.

When Toussaint saw the water coming into the boat, his panic turned into a full-blown frenzy. He left his post at the rudder and stepped forward, crying out to his God for mercy. The leaders of the expedition were on the shore watching events unfold and couldn't believe what they were seeing. They tried shouting orders and shooting their guns into the air to get the attention of Toussaint and his crew. The leaders wanted the men to get their navigator under control, but howling wind and the vast distance muted the shouts and gunshots.

As the little boat filled with water, valuable supplies were lifted by the current and started to float away. The other passengers were too busy to notice, screaming at Toussaint to snap out of it and to get back to navigating the boat and Toussaint was too busy screaming and crying. It was only after one of crew threatened to shoot the hysterical navigator did Toussaint finally calm down go back to his place at the rudder to work and save the boat.

At some point during all the madness, young Sacagawea had noticed that some of the important cargo they were carrying was floating away, back down the river that they were travelling up. Boxes of medicine, goods for trading, and pertinent documents were about to be lost forever, dooming the mission barely after it had started.

While making sure that she and the baby strapped to her back didn't fall into the river as the boat continued to rock violently from the wind and the waves, Sacagawea calmly went about recovering the lighter items before they floated out of reach. Even as the men around her shouted at and argued with each other,

Sacagawea stayed quietly focused on doing what was within her power to make their mission a success.

"In short," wrote one of the group's leaders a couple of days later, "[we almost lost] every article indispensably necessary to further the views, or insure the success of the enterprise…The Indian woman, to whom I ascribe equal fortitude and resolution, with any person onboard at the time of the accident, caught and preserved most of the light articles which were washed overboard."[2]

Just in time, Sacagawea was able to pull out most of the lighter items that had gone into the water, including vital packages of medicine, various scientific instruments, and the personal journals of the group's two leaders: Meriwether Lewis and William Clark.

---

[2] Quotation: http://ngm.nationalgeographic.com/ngm/0302/feature4/fulltext.html

The two men were thankful to Sacagawea for her quick thinking. Clark in particular was amazed by her controlled actions and the good judgment she showed while everyone around her was panicking. She was able to rescue several irreplaceable items in the midst of a raging storm while still keeping herself and her baby safe. Lewis and Clark decided that the best way to honor her quick thinking and good judgment would be to name that branch of the Musselshell River after her. Some two hundred years later it is still known as Sacagawea River.

The men were starting to realize what an incredible young woman they had invited along with them on this historic journey, and it wouldn't be the last time that they would find themselves feeling thankful for having invited Sacagawea to accompany them.

Sacagawea is one of the few Native Americans that most modern day Americans have heard of, but one whom they tend to know little about. Other than perhaps seeing her face on a coin or knowing that she travelled with Lewis and Clark, few people know about all the valuable contributions that she made to Lewis and Clark's mission of exploring the American West. They don't know how her words, actions, and knowledge helped the members of the Corps of Discovery to be successful in their journey.

The only woman to travel with Lewis and Clark, Sacagawea would eventually accompany the men for some 5,000 miles, starting from her home in Fort Mandan, North Dakota, and going over the Rocky Mountains to the Pacific Ocean. She also made the return trip with them.

On the trip, Sacagawea would get to see things that no one from her tribe had ever seen before and would be reunited with long lost relatives. Her contributions would keep the travelers healthy and protected as they navigated the uncharted wilderness. She would even help them to establish friendly relations with the Native American tribes that they met along the way.

As a teenaged bride living in the early part of the nineteenth century, Sacagawea didn't have a lot of control over her own life. She didn't get to choose where she lived or who she married. She wasn't allowed to decide what profession she would learn or how she would spend any money she might earn. But despite living in a world that treated her more like property than a real person, this young woman realized that she could decide how she would react to each of the many difficult situations that she was placed in.

Throughout her life, Sacagawea showed herself to be a person with good judgment who could adapt herself and do well wherever she was and whomever she was with.

There are so many ways to think of Sacagawea. Some see her as a young mother trying to find her way home; some imagine her as a wise Native American guide showing American explorers though her homeland, and still others visualize her acting as an ambassador who helps bring peace to different groups of people. But perhaps Sacagawea can best be understood if she is seen through the eyes of the men who travelled those 5,000 miles with her over a period of some two years. Those men saw her, not as a weak young girl, but as a steadying influence in their lives and as a person who gave them confidence and joy in times of danger and uncertainty. Sacagawea rose above what was typically expected of women in her day.

But things weren't always so joyful in Sacagawea's life - when she was just twelve years old she had to deal with an immense and unexpected change, one that would end up taking her far away from the only family and home that she had ever known.

Chapter 1: The Early Life of Sacagawea

The woman we know as Sacagawea was born in the late 1700s. Because she was born into a culture that didn't keep written records of births and deaths, no one can say with one hundred percent certainty just when she was born. We do know that she was still a teenager when she met Lewis and Clark in 1804, so it is most likely that she was born sometime between 1786 and 1789. Most researchers like to use the year 1788, which would make her about sixteen or seventeen when she made her journey with Lewis and Clark.

Sacagawea was born into the Lemhi Shoshone tribe in modern-day Idaho. Her father was a chief, and even though she was the chief's daughter it doesn't seem that Sacagawea received any particular treatment. Like most Native American girls her age, Sacagawea likely learned how to do hard work from the time she was young. Her tribe, the Lemhi Shoshone, was also known as "Agaidika", which meant "Salmon Eaters". They got this nickname because the people of the tribe fished and ate the salmon that swam through the upper Salmon River in Idaho. It is easy to picture young Sacagawea working alongside her mother and the other women of the tribe, cleaning out the day's catch and preparing it into a tasty meal for their families.

Young Sacagawea may have also learned how to build and repair the teepees that the Shoshone lived in, as well as how to break them down and set them back up each time the tribe moved from one location to another. The tribe periodically had to move from place to place, usually whenever they needed to find a new source for food or when they were having problems with a nearby tribe.

For thousands of years before American settlers arrived, Native American tribes lived all across North America. They hunted, fished, had weddings, raised children, worshipped their gods and fought wars with other tribes. But their way of doing things began to change during the 1600s, when European colonists starting arriving on their lands.

Some Native Americans began to realize that these European colonists might be a threat to their traditional way of life, so they suggested that all the different tribes should stop fighting with each other and should band together. If they could put aside their differences, they might be able to guarantee their own survival. But because of long-standing problems and lots of bad blood between the tribes and peace agreements they made usually didn't last for too long.

Centuries later, the tense situations that traditionally existed between different tribes hadn't changed much. For example, in Idaho, where Sacagawea was born, the Shoshone often found themselves fighting with the nearby Hidatsa people (and with the Hidatsa's allies the Mandan people).

The Hidatsa used rifles (which they got from Europeans) both to hunt bison and to fight against their enemies. In the year 1800, one battle between the Shoshone and the Hidatsa raged near the village where Sacagawea was living. The Hidatsa warriors attacked the Lemhi Shoshone people and rode through their lands, wreaking havoc. As the battle dragged on, one Shoshone after another was killed by Hidatsa bullets. The dead included several men, women, and young boys.

It can be hard to comprehend the terror of a twelve year old girl like Sacagawea as she hides from the violence that explodes around her and witnesses firsthand awful cries of pain and death. Somehow young Sacagawea managed to avoid getting shot, but she saw plenty of terrible things.

As she saw people she knew dying in the battle with the Hidatsa, Sacagawea had no way of knowing that her own life was about to change drastically.

As she was hiding, she was found by a group of Hidatsa warriors. The warriors kidnapped her and several other young Shoshone girls and took them far away from their homes. At just twelve years of age, Sacagawea was forced to leave to the only people and life that she had ever known and was made to live as a slave for the Hidatsa.

As part of the consequences of being taken from her family, Sacagawea would have to get used to a new culture and a new language. She was taken to the land now known as North Dakota - the place that would become her new home. She would spend the next year or so of her life working in the fields of the Hidatsa and Mandan people.

It was in this new Hidatsa culture that Sacagawea seems to have received her name. While some people think that her name has a Shoshone background, "Sacagawea" (pronounced with a soft "g") is actually a Hidatsa word that means "bird woman".

Young Sacagawea couldn't control her circumstances. Even if she had wanted to, she couldn't stop the wars that led to her being captured, and she couldn't bring back her friends and family members who had died. All she could do was try to adapt to her new circumstances and to make a success of this new life she found herself in. Although after being taken away from her family Sacagawea surely spent many nights crying herself to sleep, there came a point when she had to admit that crying lonely tears wouldn't change her circumstances and that she would have to make the best of her life as it was.

Soon after being kidnapped and forced to work for the Hidatsa and Mandan people, Sacagawea was once again forced to deal with a life-changing experience. At some point between surviving the battle with the Hidatsa in 1800 and meeting Lewis and Clark in 1804, Sacagawea was given in marriage to a French-Canadian fur trapper named Toussaint Charbonneau.

Although not a lot is known about Charbonneau, from all accounts he wasn't a terrifically great guy. Sacagawea was one of two wives that Charbonneau got from the Hidatsa-Mandan people, and it looks like he may have gotten them as part of a trade, a purchase, or in the payment of a gambling debt. In any case, it doesn't seem like love was the main reason motivation for Toussaint and Sacagawea's marriage.

Toussaint Charbonneau spoke French (his native language) and the Hidatsa language (which he had learned trading furs with the tribe). Sacagawea, for her part, spoke her native Shoshone language and the Hidatsa language of her kidnappers. By the time Lewis and Clark's group arrived in November of 1804, Sacagawea had been with Charbonneau for some time, at least long enough to be roughly six months pregnant with their child. She was approximately sixteen or seventeen by then, and her husband was at least 20 years older.

Lewis and Clark had already spent about six months travelling westward from Missouri by the time they met Sacagawea and Toussaint. They arrived in North Dakota in November of 1804. Because it was so difficult and dangerous to travel during the winter, Lewis and Clark decided to build a camp in North Dakota – which they called Fort Mandan - and to spend the winter near the Native Americans they met there.

It was on February 11 of the following year that Sacagawea gave birth to her and Toussaint's son. They named him "Jean

Baptiste". The process of giving birth to Jean Baptiste had been difficult for Sacagawea, possibly because she was so young, and a local Native American woman ended up feeding her a crushed rattlesnake rattle to help the birth process along. To the surprise of the explorers, the traditional remedy seems to have worked.

Lewis and Clark were there when Sacagawea gave birth to Jean Baptiste, and they wrote about it in their journals. Because Shoshone women were often called "Snake squaws", "squaw" being a word for woman, Lewis and Clark often referred to Sacagawea as "the Snake squaw" or "Charbonneau's woman" in their private journals.

Meriwether Lewis and William Clark had been sent west by President Thomas Jefferson to get to know more about the land that the United States had acquired as part of the Louisiana Purchase. The land transferred under the Louisiana

Purchase in 1803 measured over 828,000 square miles and the United States nearly doubled in size after the deal.

The men were supposed to see if there was any sort of water passage connecting the two coasts. Jefferson also asked them to explore what kinds of opportunities there might be for making money and how difficult future westward expansion would be. The men were also expected to make maps and to establish peaceful relations with the Native Americans they met. During their trip, the team (made up mainly of soldiers) would have to deal with flash floods, extreme temperatures, food shortages, and – worst of all – seemingly endless swarms of mosquitos.

There was some doubt about how the tribes of Native Americans along the way would feel about seeing a group of more than thirty white men, all armed with knives and guns, walking through their land. Would the Native Americans refuse to help the travelers? Worse yet, would they feel threatened and attack the white men?

To make sure that they could pass safely through the new land, Lewis and Clark knew that they would need to find some interpreters who would communicate with the different tribes. In particular, they needed some interpreters who could speak the Shoshone language. Why was it so important to find someone who spoke the Shoshone language?

Lewis and Clark would stay on the Missouri River, and its tributaries as long as they could, but they knew that eventually they would have to cross over the Rocky Mountains on foot. Crossing the Rockies would be almost impossible without horses, but there was no way to fit any horses onto their boats for the first part of the trip. So Lewis and Clark would need the help of the Shoshone people, who lived in the Bitterroot Mountains (part of the Rockies) to get horses that could carry them safely over the large mountain range.

Imagine how pleased Lewis and Clark were when they arrived at North Dakota and met Charbonneau and Sacagawea. Clark wrote in his journal: "A French man by Name Charbonneau, who Speaks the Big Belley (Hidatsa) language visit us, he wished to hire & informed us his 2 Squars (squaws) were Snake Indians, we engau (engaged) him to go on with us and take one of his wives to interpret the Snake language."[3]

Lewis and Clark saw how valuable two interpreters who spoke Hidatsa and Shoshone would be, so they invited both of them to come along. But there was still a slight problem – neither Sacagawea nor her husband Toussaint could speak English. So how could Lewis and Clark possibly tell them what to say to the tribes they met? They would have to set up a long chain of communication that

---

[3] Quotation: http://en.wikipedia.org/wiki/Sacagawea

would include one of their men, Private Francois Labiche.

Private Labiche could speak English and French. Lewis and Clark would give a message in English to Labiche, who would then translate it into French for Toussaint. Toussaint would then translate it into Hidatsa for Sacagawea, who would finally translate it into Shoshone when the time came to ask the tribe for horses. Then Sacagawea would translate the tribe's answer back for Toussaint, who would translate it for Labiche, who would finally translate it for Lewis and Clark.

Lewis and Clark initially invited Toussaint Charbonneau and his wife Sacagawea along solely for their ability to translate. But as the months and years went by, the men would learn to appreciate all that Sacagawea had to offer, and they would also come to love her son Jean Baptiste. William Clark especially would come to view Jean

Baptiste – or "little pomp" as he called him – as a son.

4

[4] Image source: http://www.kshs.org/exhibits/blc/graphics/sacagawea.jpg

After spending a long winter in modern-day North Dakota, the group finally prepared to leave the following spring. Charbonneau left behind his second wife, Otter Woman, and prepared his family for the long trip. Sacagawea had never travelled so far in her young life, and as far as she knew no one from her tribe had ever seen the Pacific Ocean with their own eyes.

While Sacagawea didn't actually have a choice in the matter – a seventeen year old mother back then was expected to go wherever her husband told her to –it seems like she was genuinely excited about travelling back through the land where she had grown up and to see what adventures she might have on the way to the Pacific coast.

Sacagawea's knowledge of plant life, animal habits, and uncharted territories would all help the Corps of Discovery in ways that they could never have imagined when they first invited her to come along. Even her presence and that of her infant son would end up helping the men in ways that they could never have predicted.

On April 7, 1805, Lewis and Clark left Fort Mandan and headed west. Sacagawea took a deep breath, strapped her baby Jean Baptiste to her back, and set off to go with them.

Chapter 2: The Career of Sacagawea

When Sacagawea left Fort Mandan with her husband, baby, and a group of American soldiers, there was no way of knowing exactly what her life would be like for the next two years. Would she run into a hostile Native American tribe and get kidnapped again, or worse? Would bad weather or a mysterious illness affect her or her family? Would their little group be able to find their way across the Rocky Mountains and all the way to the Pacific? And if they made it to the coast, would they ever be able find their way home again?

All of these questions and more filled Sacagawea's mind with each step of the journey - at least in the beginning. But as the first few days and weeks went by, the group settled into a difficult yet steady routine. Each morning the group would move as far ahead as the scouts had explored. Some of the men would walk onshore while others would stay with their precious cargo in the small little boats, called "pirogues". If the water of the Missouri River was shallow and rocky or if the current was too powerful, then sometimes the men walking on shore would tie ropes to the boats and use all their strength drag the boats upriver.

It was about five weeks after leaving Fort Mandan, on May 14, 1805, when Sacagawea saved the day by recovering the papers and bundles of medicine that had been washed overboard during the storm. Lewis and Clark couldn't help but notice the contrast between this young woman and her supposedly experienced husband. Where he panicked, she kept a cool head. Where he thought only of saving himself, she protected her baby and saved valuable items for the mission. It wasn't long before Clark and Sacagawea developed a particularly close friendship.

The men of the Corps took turns walking along the shores the Missouri, and when it was Clark's turn Sacagawea often offered to walk alongside him. The problem of language kept the two from having extremely deep conversations, but they were still able to point out new things to each other and laugh at little Jean Baptiste and the things he did.

Clark grew to truly respect Sacagawea and to love her dear son Jean Baptiste. He called Jean Baptiste "my little dancing boy" and more than once communicated to Sacagawea that he would be willing to raise Jean Baptiste as his own to make sure that the boy received a first rate education.

As the special friendship between Clark and Sacagawea grew the rest of the group began to appreciate the Shoshone girl in different ways. On more than one occasion, Sacagawea used her knowledge to make the lives of the soldiers a little more comfortable. For example, she had intimate knowledge of which plants could be used for food and which could be used for medicine. She showed the explorers a plant called a prairie turnip which could be eaten. The men grew to like the food so much that they gave it a nickname: "white apple". She also introduced the men to wild licorice and showed them how to dig up artichokes that had been buried by mice for the winter.

As the group of cross country travelers neared Shoshone territory, both on their way to and from the Pacific, Sacagawea was able to point out shortcuts to them that made the trip easier. The advice and confidence Sacagawea gave made the weary men feel happy about the progress that they were making and made them feel sure of what they were accomplishing.

After receiving one particular piece of information from the young Shoshone squaw, Lewis wrote that the "information has cheered the spirits of the party." And Clark later mentioned how much Sacagawea's guidance had meant to him. He wrote: "[Sacagawea], who has been of great service to me as a pilot through this country, recommends a gap in the mountain more south, which I shall cross."[5]

The guidance provided by Sacagawea and her help in finding food was one thing. But she never forgot that she had originally been invited on the trip with one specific job in mind – as an interpreter. When the time came, she would be expected to interpret between the Corps of Discovery and the Shoshone people and to try to get horses for the explorers. In August of 1805, Sacagawea got her chance to prove her real value to the mission.

---

[5] Quotations: http://www.biography.com/people/sacagawea-9468731

On August 17 of that year, the small group of explorers met up with members of the Shoshone tribe near the Lemhi Pass, near the modern day border between Montana and Idaho. Would the Shoshone listen to Sacagawea, the teenaged girl who had been taken from them more than five years before? Or would they see her as a traitor and refuse to help the people she travelled with?

As the group moved closer to Shoshone territory, Clark wrote of Sacagawea's happiness at being in familiar surroundings once again: "The interpreter and Squar who were before me at some distance danced for the joyful Sight, and She made signs to me that they were her nation."[6] Happy to be once again in her homeland and about to meet her own people, Sacagawea couldn't help but feel optimistic. But when she was finally able to meet up with the members of her Shoshone tribe, she wasn't

---

[6]   Quotation: http://www.biography.com/people/sacagawea-9468731

prepared for the emotional welcome she received.

First, Sacagawea had a touching reunion with a girl of about her same age. It turned out that the girl had also been kidnapped by the Hidatsa warriors on the same day as Sacagawea, but the other girl was able to escape her captors and to make her way back to her own tribe. Seeing the two women reunited made both the travelers and the Native Americans alike tear up. But an even more emotional reunion was yet to come.

Sacagawea and her fellow travelers were invited to meet the chief of the Shoshone people, and when he stepped forward there was a gasp and a cry as he and Sacagawea recognized each other. The chief was none other than Cameahwait – Sacagawea's own brother.

The two shared tears of joy as they embraced and talked about all that had happened in the five years since they had been separated. Sacagawea tried to interpret his words for the others, but she kept trying as she tried to speak from all the intense emotions she was feeling. She was proud to introduce her brother the chief to his infant nephew Jean Baptiste and to her husband Toussaint. Lewis and Clark had hoped that bringing Sacagawea along on their journey might help them to get horses from the Shoshone people, but they had no idea that in doing so they would get to be part of a special reunion like this one.

The time eventually came for the travelers to ask for the Chief's help, and Sacagawea's brother was more than happy to donate the horses the team needed to them. He was so happy to have been reunited with his sister that he promised that would help do what he could to help them continue on to the Pacific. After exchanging a few more tender words, the party of travelers continued on towards their goal of being the first representatives of the President of the United States to reach the Pacific coast.

As the party travelled over the Rocky Mountains and suffered through cold weather, Sacagawea and her charming little boy kept everyone's spirits high. But as the party descended the other side of the vast mountain range and met one tribe of Native Americans after another, everyone began to notice something surprising –the tribes they met weren't suspicious of the men and weren't acting hostile towards them.

While it may have been easy to think that the tribes were simply too intimidated by the travelers' guns to get violent or that they had been dazzled by the excellent work of the interpreters, the real reason for the easy and peaceful dealings soon became clear – it was all due to having Sacagawea and her baby Jean Baptiste in the party with them.

Clark wrote his observations on the matter: "[Sacagawea], we find, reconciles all the Indians, as to our friendly intentions – a woman with a party of men is a party of peace."[8] The various tribes of Native Americans knew if that a group of men was looking for a fight they would never bring a woman and a small child along with them. So whenever the explorers walked into a camp, any fears that the Native Americans may have had

---

[8]   Quotation: http://www.biography.com/people/sacagawea-9468731

about their intentions immediately disappeared when they saw Sacagawea's peaceful smile and heard her baby's infectious laugh. The mere presence of Sacagawea and Jean Baptiste was enough to help the mission avoid trouble just about any place the group traveled to.

By November of 1805, just about six months after leaving their home in North Dakota, Sacagawea, Toussaint, and Jean Baptiste reached Oregon along with the Corps of Discovery. At first, Sacagawea was told that she should stay at the camp, but when she heard that the group was going to have a look at a beached whale, she made it clear that there was no way she would stay behind. She had travelled too far to get this close to the Pacific Ocean to not see it. Clark expressed her reaction this way: "She had traveled a long way with us to see the great waters, and that now that monstrous fish was also to be seen, she thought it very hard she could not be permitted to see either."[9]

9   Quotation: http://www.biography.com/people/sacagawea-

The men finally agreed to let her go along.

It was near modern-day Astoria, Oregon that Sacagawea was allowed to do something that had never before been done on United States soil – she was allowed to vote on a decision that a group of men were making. In this case, the decision had to do with where the group should build their camp for the winter. In a time where only rich white men were allowed to vote, the fact that Sacagawea – a young Native American woman – was

9468731

10   Image:
http://www.lizzarddesign.com/sacagawea/journey/images/ocian.j
pg

able to vote equally with the rest was a real step forward. In fact, another hundred years or so would pass before women all across the United States would be able to vote as freely as Sacagawea did that winter in Oregon.

After the winter of 1805 passed, the group began to make the long journey back to civilization. The roughly 2,500 miles they had to travel took quite some time to cover – about six months or so. Late the following year (1806) the tired travelers said goodbye to Sacagawea and Toussaint and left them in Fort Mandan, where they had first met. Little Jean-Baptiste was nearly two years old by this time, and saying goodbye to him was extraordinarily difficult for all of the travelers, especially for Clark.

The Corps of Discovery was thankful to Toussaint and Sacagawea for their fine work. But as was the custom in those days, Toussaint (as the man of the house) was the only one who officially received a reward for his actions. He received 320 acres of land and a cash sum totaling a little over $500. For all her hard work, Sacagawea received nothing.

But in a touching letter addressed to the family, Clark wrote: "[Sacagawea] deserved a greater reward for her attention and services on that rout that we had in our power to give her… As to your little Son (my boy Pomp) you well know my fondness of him and my anxiety to take him and raise him as my own child." Clark also extended a special invitation for the family to spend some time with him in St Louis.

Together with her husband and son, Sacagawea had travelled further than anyone of her tribe ever had. She had seen things that people back home would have trouble believing, and more importantly she had revealed her true character as someone who even in the face of huge challenges and dire circumstances could use good judgment and quick thinking.

But after nearly two years of having adventures in the wilderness, could Sacagawea simply go back to living as she had before? Or would her new desire for adventure be too hard for her to ignore?

Chapter 3: The Later Life of Sacagawea

Sacagawea and Toussaint returned to their home territory in North Dakota sometime during the year 1806. There is not a lot of information available about how they felt as they tried to go back to living a simple life with the same old routine day after day. Instead of meeting new tribes and riding boats down river rapids, they had to be content with making a simple dinner and trading with the people around them. Instead of investigating whether or not the fat of a dead whale could be made into candles and enjoying the right of voting as an equal, Sacagawea essentially had to go back to the life as a "stay at home mom" while her husband went back to focusing on his career of trapping. In the meantime, young Jean Baptiste kept on getting bigger and bigger.

By 1809, both Toussaint and Sacagawea felt that it was time for a change. They had been living for the past three years with the Hidatsa people, but now that Jean Baptiste was growing up Sacagawea had to admit that any education she could give him would be limited. Clark had promised the boy a first class schooling, so Sacagawea and Toussaint decided to see if taking Clark up on his offer would give their son a better life.

They would move to St. Louis, Missouri, a big city with formal schools, and they would take up farming instead of trapping. So in 1809 the small family made the long trip to St. Louis where they were reunited with William Clark.

It's not hard to imagine how happy that reunion must have been. When Clark had last seen Jean Baptiste, he was just a little toddler. But now Clark was greeted by the sight of a five year old energetic boy. After they had finished hugging each other and once the tears had finally stopped falling, the adults doubtless reminisced about their great adventure and talked excitedly about all the happy times they had shared during their trip to the Pacific. And because it was also in 1809 that Meriwether Lewis shocked the country when he committed suicide, it is also likely that the three took some time to think and reflect on all that the great man Lewis had accomplished in his time on the Earth.

When Clark had expressed his interest during the trip in helping his "little dancing boy", he wasn't making empty promises. The former explorer was doubtless thrilled when Sacagawea and Toussaint came to St. Louis to see him and brought their little boy John Baptiste with them. Clark immediately set about trying to make the family comfortable. He found a house with some land for Toussaint to farm and made the arrangements for a boarding school to give Jean Baptiste the promised first rate education.

Sacagawea and Toussaint tried to settle down into their new life as farmers, but after some time has passed it became clear that farming wasn't Toussaint's strong suit. He had made a name for himself as a wandering trapper, and it seemed like he had a difficult time staying settled in one place just taking care of some land. So when Toussaint heard about an opportunity to go on a fur trading expedition with the Missouri Fur Company, the French-Canadian trapper couldn't pack his bags fast enough.

For her part, Sacagawea likely felt somewhat torn. She had certain responsibilities as a mother now and she wanted what was best for Jean Baptiste. It is a hard thing for any mother to leave he child in the care of another person while she goes off to work. She trusted Clark and knew he would care for Jean Baptiste the best he could, but maternal instincts are strong.

However, she couldn't help but think fondly about all the adventures that she had while travelling with Lewis and Clark. Those experiences had convinced her that there was a whole world out there to be explored, and new things to be discovered. So that is how sometime in the year 1810 or 1811 Sacagawea and Toussaint left St. Louis to go on the fur trading expedition. They left Jean Baptiste in the care of Clark while they were away. The plan was for him to receive his education until his parents came back to see him once their expedition was finished.

But nobody could have known what would actually happen - that Sacagawea would never come home from that trip and would never see Clark or her son Jean Baptiste again.

In 1812, Sacagawea gave birth to a beautiful baby daughter named Lizette. But shortly after having her daughter, it became clear that something was wrong with Sacagawea. She was suffering from some kind of a strange fever, (some think Typhoid) and she was getting sicker and sicker. On December 20, 1812, at the age of 24, Sacagawea died. She was at Fort Lisa in the area now known as North Dakota, having returned to her home territory to try and recover from her illness.

No one had thought that Sacagawea would die on that trip. She was simply supposed to go and wander for a time with Toussaint and then return to St. Louis to visit Jean Baptiste and to tell Clark all about her adventures. She was supposed to live a long life and see her children grow up and use their own spirit of exploration to meet new people and to see new places. Instead, Sacagawea died of some kind of fever far away from the people she loved.

Toussaint didn't know what to do with his infant daughter. Returning to St. Louis, he agreed to give Clark legal custody of both of the children. Toussaint ended up living well into his eighties, dying sometime in the year 1843.

Sacagawea's children Jean Baptiste and Lizette received lots of affection and fatherly attention from Clark. Clark went on to marry twice and to have many children, so the house was always full of love and laughter. Although Jean Baptiste went on to live an adventurous and successful life, nothing is said about Lizette. This silence about her life makes many scholars think that she probably got sick and died while she was still terribly young.

Jean Baptiste was famous around the country, and everyone loved to talk about "the infant boy who travelled with Lewis and Clark". After he finished school, he became friends with a German prince who invited him to spend some time in Europe. Jean Baptiste spent six years living in palaces and dining with kings and queens and eventually learned to speak four different languages. In 1829, Jean Baptiste decided to go back to the United States and live out his life in the Wild West. He worked as a hotel clerk, as a gold miner, a trail guide, and a judge before finally dying on May 16, 1866 at the age of 61 after fighting pneumonia.

Some people think that Sacagawea outlived her son and daughter and didn't die until 1884, at almost one hundred years of age. While that would be wonderful if it were true, the available evidence shows that this extraordinary young woman did indeed die in 1812, leaving behind her seven year old son and an infant daughter. Some later researchers interviewed older Native Americans who spoke of a woman named "Porivo". Porivo had often spoken of a journey that she had made with some white men, which made these researchers think that "Porivo" might just be another name used by Sacagawea.

But journals written in 1812 and the official custody transfer papers of Jean Baptiste seem to make it clear that Sacagawea was long dead by 1884. In fact, William Clark himself wrote that she was one of the members of the Corps who had died by the year 1826.

Sacagawea had touched the lives of the people that she traveled with, including William Clark. Clark had developed a deep love for Native Americans, in no small part thanks to having known Sacagawea and in having raised her son as his own. He helped Lewis as the Governor of Louisiana Territory and eventually as a Governor himself, in Missouri. He was later appointed as Superintendent of Indian Affairs by President Monroe. His deep respect for Native Americans was seen in the way he tried to help them to preserve their culture and heritage and to give them immunizations against common diseases of the day.

The life of Sacagawea had seen so many changes: kidnapped at age twelve; given in marriage shortly after to a strange man more than twice her age; surviving a difficult childbirth; taking a newborn on a cross country trip; more than one tearful reunion; and finally trying to return to a normal life after her adventures. But during each of these massive and unexpected life changing events, Sacagawea always adapted herself to her new circumstances and tried to make the best of them.

Conclusion

Sacagawea was a truly extraordinary person. When she was giving an overwhelming assignment – to convince the Shoshone tribe to provide horses for foreign explorers – she was able to carry it out. Thanks to her detailed knowledge of plants and animals on the route she was able to show the men new sources of food and medicine that they had never known about. Her experience as a girl living in the area also let her guide them through key areas and to find the best ways to reach their destination.

A lot was asked of Sacagawea, and in every single instance she was able to complete her task. And as was the case when the boat almost tipped over and spilled its precious cargo, she had the presence of mind to work for the success of the mission while others were bickering among themselves or feeling overwhelmed by conditions that were out of their control.

Because this young girl was able to accomplish so much in a time when women weren't really respected, it isn't surprising to see that she became a role model for the Women's Suffrage movement of the early 20th century. Some of the women who talked about Sacagawea tried to make her seem like more of a leader than she was as if the truth about her wasn't good enough. But in any case Americans all across the country were able to learn more about her fascinating life and her large contribution to the Lewis and Clark expedition.

Decades later, President Bill Clinton and his wife Hillary were proud to once again draw the country's attention to Sacagawea. Under President Clinton's oversight, Sacagawea was commemorated on a special $1 coin that was printed to look like it was made of gold. Because no pictures from Sacagawea's time exist of her, no one can say exactly what she looked like. But a young woman from the Shoshone tribe was chosen to model for her and everyone was happy with the result. When the coin was released, Hillary Clinton said: "The Sacagawea coin honors an extraordinary woman who helped shape the history of our nation and preserves her important legacy for future generations."[11]

12

[11] Quotation: http://www.biography.com/people/sacagawea-9468731   Quotation:

President Clinton also made Sacagawea an Honorable Sergeant in the Regular Army thanks to her efforts during the nearly two year, 5,000 trek from modern-day North Dakota to Oregon and back.

The Lewis and Clark expedition was unique in many ways but especially in the way that the members of the group were treated. An African-American slave named York was also allowed to vote the same as Sacagawea. In a situation where the normal rules of society didn't apply, there were plenty of surprises. When given the chance to shine, Sacagawea used her sound judgment to make significant contributions to the mission and to the health of the explorers. When all the restrictions that normally held her back were lifted, she proved that women were creatures capable of adaptability and critical thinking.

The explorers were amazed at how Sacagawea was able to find contentment with things as basic as food and trinkets. They may have assumed that she was a simple girl, but her wise actions and advice proved that she was a mature person who had simply never been given the opportunity to demonstrate he abilities. She served as a good lesson for Lewis and Clark not to place limitations on someone just because they come from a different culture than us or because they are not the same sex as we are.

A historian named Carolyn Gilman wrote the following about Sacagawea: "[Her] experiences may have made her one of those people permanently stuck between cultures, not entirely welcome in her new life nor able to return to her old."[13] And while Sacagawea divided her time between the Shoshone, Hidatsa, French-Canadian, and American cultures, she also used her unique experiences to help

---

[13]   Quotation: http://www.biography.com/people/sacagawea-9468731

these different groups to understand each and work with each other.

If Sacagawea had not died at the young age of 24, who knows what good she could have accomplished between the rival Native American tribes and the steady move westward of American settlers.

The story of Sacagawea is that of a young mother trying to find her way home. She left home as a seventeen year old bride who could speak Shoshone, and she came back a legend. While some people may try to glamorize what she did, the truth is enough. She exceeded everyone's expectations of her, made friends with people from hugely different cultures, and adapted to every new circumstance that she found herself in.

Sacagawea is a truly superb example of what a person can accomplish when all prejudices and limitations placed on them are removed, and the person gets a chance to show what they are really made of.

Made in the USA
Monee, IL
04 January 2024

51130991R00036